Third Wednesday Poets

An Australian Women's Poetry Anthology

Louise Berry – l.e.berry, linda ruth brooks,
Gail Hennessy, Rina Robinson, Jo Tregellis

'Third Wednesday Poets' © Copyright; 2013

© Louise Berry - l.e.berry, © linda ruth brooks, © Gail Hennessy,
© Rina Robinson, © Jo Tregellis

All rights reserved. Copyright of all material in this book remains with the poets. Without limiting the rights under copyright reserved above, no part of this work/publication may be reproduced, stored in or introduced into a retrieval system, or transmitted, in any form or by any means (electronic, mechanical, print, photocopying, recording or otherwise), without the prior written permission of the copyright owner.

Poetry/Australian

ISBN: 978-0-6482985-5-7

A copy of this book can be found in the National Library of Australia

Art Images: © linda ruth brooks
Cover photography: © Louise Berry - l.e.berry, © linda ruth brooks, © Gail Hennessy,
© Rina Robinson, © Jo Tregellis,
© Lance Hennessy

Contact: thirdwednesdaypoets@gmail.com

Disclaimer: While all care has been taken, Third Wednesday Poets and all individuals concerned accept no responsibility for the opinions of contributors or errors of interpretation during the publication process.

This book is available from www.amazon.com,
online bookstores and retail outlets.

Contents

FOREWORD vi
   Louise Berry (l.e. berry) vi
INTRODUCTION vii
   David Musgrave vii
   Mark Liston viii
ABECEDARIAN 1
   Waiting for Wednesday Poets - Jo Tregellis 2
   Always Sceptical - l.e. berry 3
   9/11 - Gail Hennessy 4
   Election – linda ruth brooks 5
   Just for the Moment - Rina Robinson 6
AUTUMN 7
   A Different Hue - l.e. berry 8
   Red and Gold - Rina Robinson 9
   Found - Gail Hennessy 10
   Seasons of the Trees - Jo Tregellis 11
   Leaves - linda ruth brooks 12
   Echoes - Rina Robinson 13
WORLD'S END 15
   Finis – linda ruth brooks 16
   World's End - Jo Tregellis 17
   The End is Nigh - l.e. berry 18
   Life is Chaos, Chaos is Life – Rina Robinson 19
   Last Solstice? - l.e. berry 20
   The Mayan Prophecy - Gail Hennessy 22
CENTO 23
   Loss - Rina Robinson 24
   Written on the Sky - Gail Hennessy 25
   No Retreat - l.e. berry 26
   A Warm Wind - Jo Tregellis 27
   False Love – linda ruth brooks 28
PAINTINGS 29
   Lady in the Garden - l.e. berry 30
   Sunday Girls - Jo Tregellis 31
   Unbroken Bond - l.e. berry 32
   Light – linda ruth brooks 33
   Gauguin's Visit - Gail Hennessy 34
   New York Movie - Jo Tregellis 35
   Picasso - Rina Robinson 36
RIDDLE POEMS 37

NATURE ... 41
- Korowa - Celebration Trees at the Ocean Baths - Gail Hennessy ... 42
- In the High Country - Jo Tregellis ... 45
- Chasm - Linda Ruth Brooks ... 46
- Scarlet - Jo Tregellis ... 47
- Nature's Gift – Rina Robinson ... 48

PLACE ... 49
- Pulbah Speaks - Jo Tregellis ... 50
- Poppies - Gail Hennessy ... 52
- So Sorry - l.e. berry ... 53
- Tsunami - linda ruth brooks ... 54
- Home - Gail Hennessy ... 56

LOOKING BACK ... 57
- Sad Yesterdays - Rina Robinson ... 58
- Water's Memory - l.e. berry ... 59
- Change of Season - Gail Hennessy ... 60
- Sonnet on Death - Jo Tregellis ... 61
- Dawn's Glory - Rina Robinson ... 62
- They Were... – linda ruth brooks ... 63

THE BOP ... 65
- Dream Holiday – linda ruth brooks ... 66
- The Gang - Gail Hennessy ... 67
- One View of Australia - Jo Tregellis ... 68
- Us or Them - l.e. berry ... 69

COLD ... 71
- So Cold - l.e. berry ... 72
- Requiem - Jo Tregellis ... 74
- Icy Voice – linda ruth brooks ... 75
- I Wonder - Rina Robinson ... 76
- A Child Remembers - Gail Hennessy ... 77

HOLIDAYS & RELIGION ... 79
- How Religion Stuffs up Holidays - Jo Tregellis ... 80
- Nothing But Crucifixions 'Til Tuesday - linda ruth brooks ... 81
- Choices - Rina Robinson ... 82
- I Remember - l.e. berry ... 83

OBSERVE ... 85
- While Broad Willows Weep – linda ruth brooks ... 86
- A Woman's Lot - l.e. berry ... 87
- The Space is Created - Jo Tregellis ... 88
- Blind Spot - Rina Robinson ... 89
- Chained – linda ruth brooks ... 90

VIEW	91
What Comes from Above - Gail Hennessy	92
Hidden Depths - l.e. berry	93
He Thinks I Sleep – linda ruth brooks	94
Blowin' in the Wind - Gail Hennessy	96
The Direction of Art - Rina Robinson	97
TANKA	99
ANSWERS TO RIDDLE POEMS	105
CENTO SOURCES FOR POEMS	106
POETS	111
l. e. berry	111
linda ruth brooks	112
Gail Hennessy	113
Rina Robinson	114
Jo Tregellis	115

FOREWORD

We were all members of the same Fellowship of Australian Writers' regional, when we started a critique poetry group, and decided to meet at the Toronto Workers' Club.

In my youth, Walter Stone (then President of FAW NSW) told me that it was important for writers and poets to get together to support and learn from each other, and the FAW was formed to promote writing, and emerging writers and poets.

When our group first met, we didn't know each other well, but over the years, and discussions about placement of commas, line breaks, and choice of words, we bonded into a supportive poetry group. This anthology shows the variety of poetry we write. Some poems have been previously published, and others appear in print for the first time.

After the angst of writing, we look back with enjoyment on our meetings and the poems we have produced. We hope you enjoy them as much as we did writing them, and putting the anthology together.

I would like to thank Lance Hennessy for taking the photographs, David Musgrave and Mark Liston for their kind words, Lake Macquarie Library at Toronto for the launch, and Magdalena Ball for agreeing to launch our anthology.

Louise Berry (l.e. berry)
Co-ordinator, Third Wednesday Poets

INTRODUCTION

David Musgrave

> Tempers awaken
> Unravelling reason
> Verbal exchanges
> Wilfully discordant
> Xylophone cacophony
> Yes, it resembles a
> Zoo
> - linda ruth brooks, 'Election'

Third Wednesday Poets is indeed a kind of poetic zoo - of form, of contemporary Australia, of the modern world and its end, of poetries past and present. Most pleasing of all is the profusion of poetic styles and forms: abecedarians, centos, ekphrasis, riddles, the bop (a kind of extended sonnet), tanka and more. Running through all this are familiar and consistent themes: the power of the wry observation, condensed into verse, to remind us of life's absurdities (Jello's advertising campaign urging their customers "to buy more of their product/to appease the Mayan gods"); the inescapable nature of loss ("your eyes crinkle/at my approach .../a memory that fades/as I tend your grave/on this windswept hill"); and landscapes transformed by poetic eyes (trees - "these alabaster tapers/keep vigil over the high country", or the ocean as "whitecaps/painting a symphony/on a seashore"). Read these poems and enjoy the verbal worlds created for you by these five poets.

> David Musgrave, prize-winning poet, author, lecturer and publisher took time out of his busy life to read our anthology and to give us his comments. We are grateful.
>
> David's poetry books are 'To Thalia' (2004), 'On Reflection' (2005), 'Watermark' (2006), 'Phantom Limb' (2010) and 'Concrete Tuesday' (2011). His poem *Coastline* won the prestigious Newcastle Poetry Prize in 2012. In 2011 his novel 'Glissando: A Melodrama' was shortlisted for the Prime Minister's Award for Fiction.
>
> David's company, Puncher & Wattmann, has published works, which have been shortlisted or won most of the major literary prizes in the country.

Mark Liston

This anthology begins with an evocative photograph. The five poets are happily crossing a road, joined in the fellowship of smiles, poetry and place. It is redolent of the famous Beatles album cover of Abbey Road; four musicians joined together for posterity- just like the five female poets that inhabit this anthology.

So to stretch the analogy further I found 'Something' 'Come Together' in these pages. Short poems written to selected Forms eg Tanka, and to selected themes eg Place is a clever idea that gives the individual poems a feeling of wholeness and a sense of egalitarian endeavour.

This is a substantial record for these five women. So I invite all intending readers to find a comfy seat, pour a hot cuppa open up a window because, maybe, 'Here Comes the Sun'. Enjoy!

Mark Liston recently won the All Poetry Competition 2013 and has completed a stint as Australian Poetry Café Poet in Newcastle. He is published widely and his first collection 'Fragile Diamonds' was published by Picaro Press also in 2013.

He says *'He is delighted to introduce this Anthology'.*

ABECEDARIAN

Abecedarian is an ancient form of poetry closely tied to religious songs and prayers.

The first line must start with 'A', each line thereafter starts with the following letter in the alphabet right through to 'Z'.

Waiting for Wednesday Poets - Jo Tregellis

Am sitting here with a
Beer on the table
Cold frothy refreshing
Dull noise of poker machines in my
Ears someone wins.
Fordy five 4 5 the bingo lady calls
Giving someone a prize
How is it that people like bingo?
Is it monotonous   awkward
Juggling five or six cards and a dot marker
Kids absent today, back at school
Ladies in the coffee lounge
Munch cakes and sandwiches
Not regarding their figures
On cue they wipe their mouths
Pursing for fresh lipstick
Questioning the date for the next meeting
Rows of empty armchairs
Surround me hoping
To be sat upon by
Underwhelmed keno players whose
Vision seeks the god-screen
With adoring intent and prayer
X marks the lucky spot   after
Years of trying finally the deity
Zeros in on their numbers

Always Sceptical - l.e. berry

Always sceptical
Because of family

Can't you see
Dancing among the leaves
Elves with their favourite
Fairies in attendance
Gyrating to unearthly music
Heard only by their ears

Initially   celestial beings
Joke at their antics
Keep themselves apart
Liking their superiority until the
Music lifts to the skies
Nudges angelic bodies to
Occasionally let the
Patter of their wings
Quietly
Reveal their joy

Showers of angel dust
Travel to the earth
Until the elves and fairies wear
Velvet capes
Woven by magic

X-rays from on high
Yield pictures of the celestial
Zodiac

9/11 - Gail Hennessy

After the twin towers fell
Before other acts of desperation
Constellations still held their place
Did we dare to believe
Even though the
Future appeared clouded
Growing strong before
Hope that would fashion
Into a rebuilding
Just as we held out our arms
Kisses soft on our lips
Like birds rising
Masking the sky with promise
No wisp of cloud on the horizon
Our dreams distant as stars
Perhaps we could re-build from the ash
Quintessential longing
Rounding desire
Simple as salt on the
Tongue
Under the roof
Vying house against home
Willing
Xenophobia defeated
Yea
Zenith to our broken dreams

Election – linda ruth brooks

Answers shrink
Bringing more questions
Coursing towards the brink
Day of 'election'
Folly joins hands with
Glory and pride
Heckling grows louder
Insinuation flies
Justice blurs
Kingship topples
Loyalty fades
Money is paramount
Nullifying need
Orators fumble
Promises abound
Questions tumble
Rhetoric is epidemic
Syntax and semantics
Tempers awaken
Unravelling reason
Verbal exchanges
Wilfully discordant
Xylophone cacophony
Yes, it resembles a
Zoo

Just for the Moment - Rina Robinson

All I was thinking
Before I got out of bed
Cute ideas
Delightful images
Entering my mind
Flying swiftly
Going around and around
Hardly staying for moments
In my head
Just for a while
Keeping to the script
Loving every
Meaningful moment
Nowhere did
Other ways
Present themselves
Quaint
Reasons for
Shedding my inhibitions
Took hold
Utterly undermining my
Virtuous values
With the
X Factor
You could be in the
Zone too

The tree and I are one
'A Different Hue'- l. e. Berry

AUTUMN

A Different Hue - l.e. berry

as leaves change colour
my heart slows
my body sheds the gaiety of youth
takes on a different hue

my feet crunch fallen leaves
dreams long held
shatter under obligations
thrust on me by death

soon the trees are naked
no history of beauty
etched on bare branches
no shelter from the elements

the skeleton of my future
stripped of illusion
gives no comfort
no hint of abundance

misery dwells in my pores
oozes out to cover
flesh devoid of life
clogs hope of change

the tree and I are one

Red and Gold - Rina Robinson

Autumn winds
Icy
Blowing from
Somewhere cold
Yet still the sun shines
And coloured leaves
Red, gold and bronze
Fall
To drift
On the wind
Into gutters
A fire hazard
That must be cleared
Making work
For somebody

Found - Gail Hennessy

early evening and raining
one leaf tugged by autumn winds
lay above a circular light
set in the pavement
lighting the path
that led to the RSL

perfectly positioned
the leaf had found its place
stem and maple shape
crimson veined with brown
rain had stuck it fast
varnished its sheen

like an illuminated letter
perfect in that moment
I took it home with me
on the lens of my camera

Seasons of the Trees - Jo Tregellis

five trees
line the road
outside my home
telling the seasons
to my soul.
bare branches
scrape the sky
long before I have time
to note the vanity
of showy leaves.
so soon
the green tinge
of jealous leaves
springs out
to remind me
that I envy their spontaneity.
full summer glory –
in the canopies' spread
of comforting shade
I rest, and
can't help but wonder.

Leaves - linda ruth brooks

Leaves
flutter and tumble,
then crunch underfoot,
from trees that have shed
their summer ballroom clothes,
sitting serenely in their dainty petticoats
of vermillion, sienna, ochre and gamboge.

Some
are ambiguous,
holding to verdant hues
that sit side by side with red,
orange, crimson, gold and aubergine
even the petite shrubs succumb to autumn;
soon the naked branches alone will reach elegantly.

Oh that we could die so beautifully,
to live again when spring whispers warmly.

Echoes - Rina Robinson

When nights are long and leaves turn gold and fall
And even simple things become some pleasure
Then may one rose still linger bold and tall
To add to winter's dreary treasure

As in the closing of each darkening day
The chapter closes, being lightly written
With time's stubborn march we must obey
And age a destiny with which we all are smitten.

Now mem'ries of those early enterprises,
Ambitions faded, yet once strong forces grew,
Then recollections of one's youth arises
To gild the saddened life that fairly flew

Heav'n grant one constant friend may prove that flower
To cheer your day in ev'ry lonely hour

Earth gave a low murmur
'Finis' – linda ruth brooks

WORLD'S END

Finis – linda ruth brooks

clocks stopped
ground shivered
birdsong changed
just a little

nothing out of the ordinary
hardly noticed

Mayans predicted
it would be big

the unexpected
should be expected

the end came quickly

Earth gave a low murmur
turned inside out
no time for conjecture
scientific analyses
or pandemonium

still there it is—
third planet from the Sun
the view from this flying saucer
shows a glowing red orb

why did I thumb a ride?
I wish I'd stayed

better the devil you know...

World's End - Jo Tregellis

the end of the world is about to happen
at least in South America
why would you believe Mayan predictions
when you can't see the demise of Australia
as you once knew it
staring you in the face

a big bang would stop the plunder
of our land
everything would go
water farms mines power

in the end
there are no winners

2

the end of the world
ho hum
better stock up on the booze
just in case I'm spared
either way I'll be happy

I could invite friends
to an enormous barbecue
or grasp the chance to feed the poor
bringing them in from highways and by ways
all leaving this earth
with a full belly
and a numbed brain

what about that eh

The End is Nigh - l.e. berry

i.
I devour headlines
read articles
believe Mayans had mystical
powers to predict

housework beckons
in vain
why spend my last hours
scrubbing

I drink tea from
fine china cups
use cake forks
and damask napkins

I burn expensive
sandalwood incense
in my special fake jewel
encrusted holders

lie on my bed
compose my thoughts
make peace with my maker
and wait

ii.
as morning sun pours
into my bedroom
I know the world
has not ended

alas
here is a new day
a new calendar
and an old mess to clean up

Life is Chaos, Chaos is Life – Rina Robinson

Prancing, advancing,
Little boy dancing,
Unfolding delights in a whole new age.
Chancing, entrancing,
Life enhancing,
Greeting adventures at each new stage.
Questioning, questing,
Youth never resting,
Assured in ambitions to which he aspires.

Learning, yearning,
Never quite earning
Respect for his offhand impromptu desires.
Passions, pleasures, prosperity, fortunes, friendships, family, ideals, dreams.
Discord, prejudice, tempest, tactics, obscurity, chaos, warfare, screams.

Dated, truncated,
Withered, humiliated,
Waiting for what, now the years are all spent.

Hard of hearing, interfering,
Biased, also domineering,
Wondering where all the treasures went.

Last Solstice? - l.e. berry

1.
The night before Midsummer
Crickets sleep under decaying leaves
Exhausted from the long day singing
Dream of tomorrow's fun

Witches   white and black   prepare
Ancient fertility rituals
Seek to please their mentors
    Increase devotees and believers

Obsessed   would-be parents
Gather courage and money
To overcome nature's perverse ways
Shattering their dreams

Tomorrow they will meet
At the appointed hour
Watch as the moon shifts
Away from the midday sun

Alas they never knew
What the Mayans knew
    When the sun rose high
Time ran out

2.
In the next dimension
All bodies fall away
No need for clothes or things
Only consciousness survives

Few remembered the journey
As the earth imploded
Scattering land and water
Into the furnace of time

If occasionally there's an idea
Of a life before the now
It's dismissed as half-baked
Memories from an ancient time

Now they live in harmony
In their home in the skies
No need for food or water
    No need for work or lies

The Mayan Prophecy - Gail Hennessy

You have to die and to know
exactly when, has to be a bonus
so prepare for your final demise.

Seasons turn with certainty
December comes with finality.
In the narrative of history
21 December 2012's a date
as good as any you're likely
to be given.

The degenerate ones can stumble
to perdition while the chosen few
will inherit a new sphere when
earth and Niburi collide.

Can astronomical alignments
and numerological formulae
predict or be the cause
of Armageddon

Jello's American manufacturers
were on a winner no worries
when they urged their customers
to buy more of their product
to appease the Mayan gods.

Sales soared as the gelatine dessert
whipped itself into mountains
of no-bake cream pies,
all presage to a sticky end.

CENTO

From the Latin word for "patchwork," the cento (or collage poem) is a poetic form made up of lines from poems by other poets. Though poets often borrow lines from other writers and mix them in with their own, a true cento is composed entirely of lines from other sources.

Early examples can be found in the work of Homer and Virgil.

Loss - Rina Robinson

As I drive to the junction of lane and highway
At the midnight in the silence of the sleep-time
Winds whisper gently while she sleeps
She walks in beauty, like the night
The unpurged images of day recede
That civilization may not sink

Come again to the place
Come live with me, and be my love
To seek new worlds
Fear no more the heat of the sun
Woman much missed, how you call to me, call to me
Absent from thee I languish still
With all my will, but much against my heart
I have desired to go

Shall I come, sweet love, to thee
As I walked out that sultry night
Well I remember how you smiled
When love with unconfined wings
A widow-bird sat mourning for her love

I looked for that which is not, nor can be
I wonder, do you feel today
The land was ours before we were the land's
The irresponsive silence of the land
By the rude bridge that arched the flood

All's over then, does truth sound bitter
Farewell, Love, and all thy laws for ever

(Sources on page 106)

Written on the Sky - Gail Hennessy

We find out the heart only by dismantling what
the heart knows. By redefining the morning,
the structure of landscape is infinitesimal
landscape softens the sharp edge of isolation
that harsh biblical country of the scapegoat.
It is winter and the stars are hidden
how quiet the bells of heaven must be, cold
with stars who cannot rhyme their brilliance
when only the moon rages.

The stars do not blow away as we do,
the heavenly things ignite and freeze
Orion bends in the northeast to tighten his sandals.
We must unlearn the constellations to see the stars
in the denominations of light.

(Sources on page 107)

No Retreat - l.e. berry

again and again
inside and out
fill every gap
intimacy's slow cocoon is spun

let's say in the shadow
we are forgetting
draw a frame around it
for the girls

her attunement
nested with shadows
as loose and slippery as rolling peas
outside, black cats glide

I'm home today
the sky's gone thin
I pull on a sweater

(Sources on page 108)

A Warm Wind - Jo Tregellis

life's troubled bubble broken
breathless, we flung us on the windy hill
bring me my chariot of fire
there is a pleasure in the pathless woods
the houses are all gone under the sea
the dancers are all gone under the hills
this is the weather the cuckoo likes
and so do I
as kingfishers catch fire, dragonflies draw flame
it's a warm wind, the west wind
full of birds' cries
and a woman is only a woman
but a good cigar is a smoke

love looks, not with the eyes
but with the mind
men seldom make passes
at girls who wear glasses
but lasting joys the man attend
who has a polished female friend

(Sources on page 109)

False Love – linda ruth brooks

She went to plain-work, and to purling brooks
Old fashioned halls, dull aunts and croaking rooks
And utterly consumed with sharp distress
As if she played unheard some tenderness
Should be to aftertime, but empty breath
As of no worth

Like one that on a lonesome road
On the hungry craving wind
She had looked for his coming as warriors come
Could the passionate past that is fled
Call back its dead

And who could play it well enough
If deaf and dumb and blind with love?
That not a heart which in his level came
Could 'scape the hail of his all-hurting aim

Love's stricken "why"
Is all that love can speak
Fade away, dissolve and quite forget
What thou amongst the trees hast never known
And let their shadows down like shining hair
While an abstract insight wakes
And love seeks better loving

(Sources on page 110)

PAINTINGS

Poems inspired by paintings, or other works of art, are known as Ekphrasis, which is a rhetorical device in which one medium of art tries to relate to another medium by defining and describing its essence and form. In doing so, it relates more directly to the audience, through its illuminative liveliness. A descriptive poem may thus highlight what is shown in a work of art, and thus may enhance the original art and so take on a life of its own through its brilliant description.

Lady in the Garden - l.e. berry
Good-bye - Margaret Olley

her Rubenesque figure
shaded by a straw hat
sits comfortable among flowers
she was wont to paint

from the chaos of her room
evocative paintings
sprung from canvases
large and small

she was the darling of the art world
      and the general public too
as an artist's model she sat
      for a select few

her death was a sad event
to those who lost a friend
and to the art world
who mourned such talent

Sunday Girls - Jo Tregellis
Sunday, Girls drying their Hair - 1912 - John Sloan

On a small Manhattan rooftop
girly curves contrast with brick angles
wind dries wet hair
washing flings about in the air
three young women so feminine
stretch to show rounded breasts
small waists and full thighs
enjoy friendship's warmth
no jealousies here
only a freedom of movement
a radiant delight
to be out of cramped apartments
on a sunny Sunday

Unbroken Bond - l.e. berry
Two Figures in a boat one standing - 2007- Norman Lloyd

I move through life
    in unexpected ways
I remember you

sometimes   I feel you
look over my shoulders
judging what I do

your voice reminds me you
    changed my nappies
have seen me naked

to others I am adult
    but to you I'll
always be a child

as I wait for my boat
    to come in
I remember you

Light – linda ruth brooks
Rainbow Trail - Greg Valeer

dim midnight hospital light
I think my waters have broken
the covers are thrown back
there's only crimson red
oh my god

                      filtered light
                      shining on
                      the secret trail
                      of my childhood
                      shadows cross the vale

fluorescent shatters
everything moves
too fast
the baby isn't moving
at all

                      the path shines
                      trees recede
                      their solid strength
                      enigmatic
                      in the dark background

theatre light blinds
gowned figures glide
swift and efficient
fighting for me
will my child live

                      subtle light
                      hues and tones emerge
                      shadows dim
                      angles soften
                      blending as one

soft dawn glow
my child lives
his raucous tone
a musical thread
of victory

Gauguin's Visit - Gail Hennessy
The Bedroom in Arles, 1888 - Vincent Van Gogh

It has become a tabernacle
the square chair with its raffia seat
each strand woven like star anise

a wood framed window
crucifix panelling.
On the wall your painting

of sunflowers – a gift
for a recipient
yet to arrive

outdoors there waits a starry night
whorled haloes spinning
in a navy sky

avenues of closed blossoms
yet to bloom, perfume
of apricots

a small bed
with two pillowcases
like sealed envelopes

paint thick as churned
cream that creases cotton
to the texture of promise

in another painting of this room
you paint the pillows
chartreuse, a truer colour perhaps

for treachery?

New York Movie - Jo Tregellis
New York Movie, 1939 - Edward Hopper

usherette stands by heavy red drapes
black strappy high heels sunk in plush carpet
her sleek uniform striped red
down blue trousers

the glow of lamps lighting the stairs
shows the gold in her hair
chin rests on one hand torch in the other
not looking at the screen

I've seen this movie many times
I'm bored
but lucky to have this job
how many people in these soft red seats
have a job?
only a few I think
they're here to escape reality
some see the same movie over and over
to fill in their lonely days
watching black and white fantasy

nearly the end
perhaps the evening session
won't be so empty

Picasso - Rina Robinson
Woman with flower - Pablo Picasso

What is this?
I know it's good
People say so.
Yet somehow I cannot
See what it is today
Maybe tomorrow

Painting is fun
When it goes right

It is frustrating
When it does not

But persevere,

Getting it right
Is the goal

I wonder if
Monet, Matisse
Or Michelangelo

Had this same problem

RIDDLE POEMS

(answers to riddles on page 105)

Rina Robinson

I am not soft and seldom pretty
you won't need me when you're dead
I may be large or small
not often witty
you need me to keep your head

l.e. berry

I am flexible and light
sometimes dry, sometimes moist
shallow but often deep
essential for communication
expressive and still
what am I?

Gail Hennessy

I transform, I hide
I change sharpness to curves
I am soft and hard
I flurry, I slant, I settle
traffic ceases, birds migrate
in my coming I bring magic
departing I am ragged
you will welcome my arrival
curse me if I stay too long.

linda ruth brooks

I burn
I am ice
I shake, rattle and roll
I rumble like thunder
I rage
...then I linger

Jo Tregellis

in a song of some fame
in a singer by another name
echoes heard in a distant vale
captured in bottles for sale

'an eagle eye vantage'
Korowa - Celebration Trees at the Ocean Baths - Gail Hennessy

NATURE

Korowa - Celebration Trees at the Ocean Baths - Gail Hennessy

It is always the lacuna
that the monument wears
that lingers,
the image that haunts
with its underlay of memory.

Ghosts that inhabit inscription
corridor the past
ancestors you carry
in the heart
in the head.

Memory that cries
to be inscribed
clamours for commemoration
to recall past histories
insists on tomorrow's tribute.

Two poles stand
striated, weathered,
recall inland forest
symbolic monuments
that spear sky, challenge easterlies
wear water breathing through wood.
Tallow timber is written
with calligraphy
marks in turned wood
ladder-climb its sheen
upright in a circle of granite
planted, capped in stainless steel.

Who will remember?
The schoolchildren who worked
to design this memorial
to ancestors, the craftsmen
who laboured, the anchors
that stitched wood to earth.

It has been a long journey
for this statement to stand
here on the surrounding space
of the ocean baths
twin symbols that embrace place.

Sheen of grey granite
in a mandala freezing
waves that circled these shores
fish and turtle abound
a celebration of Awabakal
and Worimi peoples.

From an eagle eye vantage
this landscape was laced
with creamed foreshores
the paddle of canoes
shoals of netted silver on the beach
stands of timber flowing to the water's edge.

Time past was measured by sun and moon
the position of seasonal stars
from sleep nights to camp site
by sooty oystercatchers, markers of tides
crustaceans and shellfish embroidered the shore.

The baths are divided from unmarked pool
by lanes where swimmers notch their laps
or race each other from end to end
there is stasis here.

It is fitting that these trees stand
guardian to children who will learn
survival skills in water,
breaststroke and backstroke,
the Australian crawl,

witness to the ghosts of men
who came back from the wars
stretched their crippled limbs
in the clemency of salt water
entered the pool on specially built ramps
felt in oceanic benediction
the solace of healing...

In the High Country - Jo Tregellis

they stand
like white asparagus spears
eucalypt regens
victims of raging flames
ten years ago

no life
no regeneration
stark against new grown trees
that wander up and down the hills

mountain ash
tall straight unknotted
valuable timber
prized medium of craftsmen
harvesting after the fire
was prohibited

the utility of their wood
lost forever
these alabaster tapers
keep vigil over the high country
and wait for hell's acolytes
to ignite the next burning

Chasm - Linda Ruth Brooks

tectonic shift   how beautiful the ravage
each layer   a foundation of eons past
colours of earth   sienna umber ochre ecru
sliced in meticulous symmetry

deep blue   quivering waters beneath
breach the gap below
deceptive   deeper than ocean's millennia
cobalt serenity   connecting two worlds

inching apart   infinitesimal shift
unseen   unnoticed by city street throngs
continents adrift
ancient pervasive unstoppable

my weary heart   at the headland
swoops low in melancholy
unable to breach
the distance too great

Scarlet - Jo Tregellis

from red sand
scarlet bracts and black peas
showed a way
for explorers

a vase in the foyer
of the Broken Hill art gallery
overflowed with vibrance

the volunteer said
she picked them from
the front of her house
a sandy nature strip

wildflowers
from an arid landscape
she gave me some seeds
wild things don't need a gardener
she said
just throw them on sandy soil
in the sunshine

I did
nothing grew

I have the memory
of its scarlet vividness
the Sturt Pea
amongst the sculpture symposium
in the living desert

Nature's Gift – Rina Robinson

Breezes
ruffling along branches
echoing whispers,
nature's harmonies,
home to birdsong

Ripples
etchings on a smooth runway,
whitecaps
painting a symphony
on a seashore

Shadows
cast into the gift of sunlight
serene, luminous,
no illusion

See; listen,
now,
within your mind,
lest your music
should fade
forever.

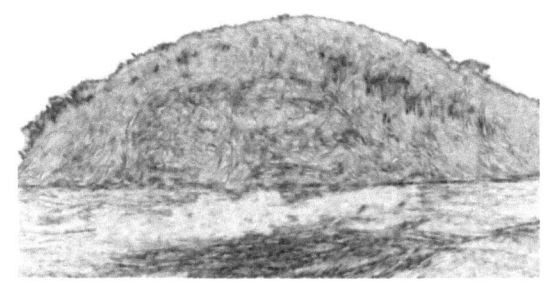

I am Pulbah, I have a pulse
'Pulbah Speaks' - Jo Tregellis

PLACE

Pulbah Speaks - Jo Tregellis

I am Pulbah.
past patriots felt my pulse
put collective fingers on it
adopted my heartbeat.

I was their dream
Utopia for flora and fauna
for feathered flights
for furred economy.

1918, they visited
in suits, ties and hats
pushed shiny shoes through my sands
willed me to thrive.

I gave spotted gums and ironbark
fed cattle and rabbits
surrendered my shells for lime
spewed my fish into nets.

vandals wrenched out
my ancient plants
rubbished cove and cave
caused me pain.

I know when you try to help
annually you scrape with gardening tools
pull at rogue bush and vine
begin again to reclaim the vision.

as sentinel of the lake
I count endless moons and suns
shelter sails from storms
gaze into night's star glory.

I will not move from here.
the patriots prayed I would prosper,
those men ahead of their time.
others could not understand.

I am an island
famed in Awabakal dreaming.
you all could know me.
I am Pulbah. I have a pulse.

Note. Pulbah Island in Lake Macquarie near Wangi Wangi was declared a Nature Reserve in 1929.

Poppies - Gail Hennessy
(for Wendy and Noel)

He retired after thirty years underground
in the mines near Cessnock
dug up his front and backyard and planted
poppies.

Not just run-of the-mill poppies
but pleated and frilled and double-petalled
with pollen like the gold he hadn't found.

You bought me two bunches
elegant on their leggy stems
left them in a blue jug on the kitchen bench.

Saffron cups of colour
ruffled pink and white
red as Flanders fields.

That night I went into John Hunter's
emergency ward
where I dreamed of poppies

imagined them overriding the drip
flowing through the cannula in my arm
flowering like opium through the blood.

So Sorry - l.e. berry

It shudders like squid ink
Over rough rocks
Hides what lies beneath

Dark clouds part
Celestial torch reveals
Horrors of unbridled rage

Water oozes over the
Wasted life knocking
Against wharf's piers

It's lonely to die
Away from home
For no real reason

Water is impersonal
As it pushes its prey
Further into the barnacles

No-one's son
The cadaver waits for someone
To know it's here

Its soul released from
The bondage of flesh

Tsunami - linda ruth brooks
Phuket, Boxing Day 2004

paradise
beautiful one day...
devastation
the next
walls of water
scrape the sky

                          waves thunder
                          tides plunder

voices scream
arms flail
reach and grasp
nature breaks open
a world upside down
lungs are bursting

                          bodies tumble
                          buildings crumble

idyll to hell
debris and chaos
tattered pages
names and images
pinned to endless boards
dead or alive?

                          distance and despair
                          in the fetid, dying air

minutes remaining on
battered mobile phones
thousands search
shelter with strangers
bloodstained torn clothes
donated by the destitute

                          gratitude and grace
                          one desire - a beloved's face

a family of five
tossed like matchsticks
and severed
two parents
three children
lost, then found

                        sweet the reunion
                        amid death and confusion

but we
in the blur
of everyday life
shiny new mobiles, but
odd little silences
pained separations

                        hearts underground
                        lost, not found

Home - Gail Hennessy

this country's too big, too sunburned
flowing with neither milk nor honey but dust clouds
its rivers choked

I picture its sweeping plains, its vast encroaching deserts
I cling to the fringe of its circling oceans, its fault lines
that fat middle girth

too many sporting heroes, too much sport, too much hype
copious celebrities whose names I don't know and don't want to,
corrupt politicians

who lie and no-one cares or votes out of office,
like Pied Pipers they have led us into wars
not of our business

still the index finger of Cape York beckons me back
to its nibbled-out gulfs, its grinning oversize Bight,
an opal refraction

I come home to a harbour more beautiful than any other,
that lassoes my heart and ties me to this land
immense in its antiquity

in the supermarket the man in blue overalls
behind me in the queue
holds my place

when I forget the milk, and says 'no worries darl
we'll all get to the same place in the end.'

How long ago was yesterday
'Sad Yesterdays' - Rina Robinson

LOOKING BACK...

Sad Yesterdays - Rina Robinson

How long ago was yesterday,
when we strolled hand in hand
on gentle verdant slopes
or sweeping sunburnt sands?

We made our solemn promises
to honour, to cherish, to nurture,
then happily came our miracle,
a likeness to you in miniature.

We were so happy then,
nothing could spoil our joy
as we watched with quiet pride
the growth of our lovely boy.

He was clever, he was popular,
we saw nothing sinister
to sully his potential
to become a young Prime Minister.

But did we let him down,
was it us that were inconsequent?
We could not foresee,
we had no presentiment.

We gave him what we could,
though he seldom asked for much.
From where came a weapon
so comforting to clutch?

Perhaps he was unhappy
perhaps a bullied child,
we never saw the pain
for our boy was never wild.

How long ago was yesterday?
We love our baby still
but how could we ever imagine
that a child of twelve could kill?

Water's Memory - l.e. berry

My emotions revealed
Under the microscope

As the water I hold
Remembers patterns

Everything is energy
Or so the scientists say

Words written on paper
Cause molecules to sync

My secret thoughts
Laid bare to the enlarged eye

Slide after slide
Tells my history

Will this ancient technology
Get the same kudos

As working out the genome
Or testing DNA

I hope it remains
In the knowledge of the few

I'd hate to see an app
Decide my destiny

Change of Season - Gail Hennessy

In this house

it is only at this time of year
that the sun slants through
windows that face north-west

illuminates the blue bathroom tiles
torches the window-sill of the kitchen.
For this part of the earth

is approaching its Spring equinox.

I remember the day you came to see
the bare bones of this half-built house.
You bought a house-warming gift

a Meyer lemon in a pot.

You climbed the makeshift stairs
exclaiming at the shafts of light.
We did not know then
.
it is only in early September

that the sun's rays fall in that
particular paradigm so
for some segmented time

those rooms dance under
its patina, enamelling
surfaces with light.

Each year since your death
September
resurrects your memory

brings you back
in exclamations of delight
look! and look!

The Spring sunshine soaks to itself
disperses warmth
your figure shimmers on the stair.

Sonnet on Death - Jo Tregellis

In time, it's said, the pain will surely fade
but aches, though dull, persist through all my days.
You sleep beneath the ash tree's ample shade
and skies show hues of all the blues and greys.

Your face, your voice, have disappeared from me,
old photographs, a poor substitute
for mother's love.   I spoke no eulogy.
Those decades ago, I was not resolute.

Of wise words and mentors there were none.
My life's much longer than yours in years.
Alas I do not have a daughter or a son
to write a sonnet for me through guilty tears.

I do believe on judgment day we rise
to reconnect love's broken, severed ties.

Dawn's Glory - Rina Robinson

When I can no longer see
I shall remember this

A lake hidden from view
With the first glimpse in the first light
There is no lapping of gentle waves
No disturbance
Only the glorious mantle of morning mist
Draping its ethereal cloak expansively.

There are vessels that make voyages
Around the world,
Their owners bringing back tales of romantic places;
There are vessels that make a Saturday voyage
To the other end if the lake,
Even they engender dramatic dialogue
At times;

But now all this is just a ghostly presence
Silent, unmoving,
A cartoon outline
Shrouded in this veil of mystery,
Not even leaving an imprint
Or reflection of itself
On the smooth mirror it rests on.

As the saffron light gilds the trees
A celestial radiance creates an aureate backdrop
Lifting the gossamer shroud gently
In a Monet impression
Of a new day of beauty.

These are things I have loved
And will remember.

They Were... – linda ruth brooks

She wore
demure backless dresses
so he could drag hot kisses
down her spine.

Throwing aside
her inhibitions
she lay with him
romped   played
as they laughed
like carefree children.

Perhaps
free of care in a way
neither had truly
been before.

Of all the places
they went together
in that moment
each was the other's
destination.

For every
tearful farewell
there was
poignant reunion.

Until the last time
when they clung together
like the lost children
they really were.

She lay beside
a couple of men
to forget him,
then she lay alone
to remember herself.

Only in her dreams,
when time had no meaning
did she see him.

THE BOP

Not unlike the Shakespearean sonnet, the Bop is a form of poetic argument consisting of three stanzas, each stanza followed by a repeated line, or refrain, and each undertaking a different purpose in the overall argument of the poem.

The first stanza (six lines) states the problem, and the second stanza (eight lines) explores or expands upon the problem. If there is a resolution to the problem, the third stanza (six lines) finds it. If a substantive resolution cannot be made, then this final stanza documents the attempt and failure to succeed.

Dream Holiday – linda ruth brooks

a holiday, oh what a dream
idyll rural diversion – just feed the pets
rippling brook, organic veg
a dainty cottage with modern conversion
seemed too good to be true
air fares paid, car and accommodation free

I knew how to respond

the website delighted with charming vistas
Oh dear, goodness me, there were sheep
I'd winded the last cranky ewe I encountered
it was butting the children, what else could I do
Oh gosh, oh golly, there were horses
I'd been traumatised for life by equine adventures
winded by an ancient draft horse, no less
who stood where I was and not where I wasn't

I knew how to respond

photos arrived by email
the glory of the housing was for paying guests
the quaint servant's quarters had no heating
no cooling for hot Queensland nights
bathroom was just up the way
Oh heavens to Betsy what could I say

I knew how to respond

The Gang - Gail Hennessy

They got bikes
young and old, got guns, got dope
got energy rampant in their thighs
under beards got tattoos
wear goggle-shields over eyes
under leather carry flick knives

where they gonna stick that anger?

they got open roads
like treacle runs quick-silver
roar and rage those machines
guttural their trajectory
ready to swallow their need
for unchecked speed. Outback
ribbons ought to tie them soft
burn that speed out of those tyres

where they gonna stick that anger?

Set up crime squads, commissions,
investigations, search warrants,
tap phones, confiscate rifles,
hand guns and pistols (ain't those the same?)
explosives, detonators, ice, hand grenades
counterfeit cash. Bust that network.

Now where they gonna stick that anger?

One View of Australia - Jo Tregellis

the land that is our country is under threat you see
from CSG exploration
soon gas holes will spread like the pox
to rival the unfaded wounds of coal massacres
there will be no attempt to rehabilitate
regenerate or even reuse these ugly scapes

a monsoon does not have enough tears for this

farmers' despair   what's beneath the soil
is not theirs   they must surrender
to the plunder and rape of the food bowl
their families are sickened by evil vapours
and residues that invade their farms
like rats spoiling pure aquifers
yet decision makers blunder on
with sightless ferocity

a monsoon does not have enough tears for this

try to make a stand
and machines and law band together
to skittle you into the earth
you cannot beat greed or devious bastards
you cannot disprove the lies of environmental surveys
you cannot do anything on your own
combined power is the only answer

a monsoon does not have enough tears for this

Us or Them - l.e. berry

others send out vibes
shunning the different
each century picks a victim
makes them unlike us
the knowing is not for anyone
who is apart from this group

if you're not one of us – go

recipient of egalitarian views
bridle in disdain
draw tradition and culture
tight like a protective coat
new ideas bring discontent
disturbs what is right and proper
titling status quo on its axis
foretelling a new doomsday

if you're not one of us – go

wireless technology abounds
easier communication they promote
yet knowing your neighbour
enough to have a chat
old fashioned behaviour
can I text you on that

if you're not one of us – go

the door closes with a snap
'So Cold' - l.e berry

COLD

So Cold - l.e. berry

she wakes to sounds of screaming
her heart pounds   hurry   hurry
her eyes flicker around
she calls   Mum   Mum

silence   then the clunk of beads
rattling rhythmically
with shuffling feet
    stop outside her door

hinges creak in protest
a nun stands in the doorway
hush   you'll wake everyone
you need your sleep for tomorrow

no kiss good night
no hand gently wiping her brow
no whispered sweet nothings
    the door closes with a snap

dawn   bleak and cold
sends shafts of grey nurse light
into the narrow room
to glint on her cheeks

a quick rap on the door
before it flings open
a different nun calls out
you need to hurry

she dresses in her allocated clothes
of a colour and style not her own
walks into the corridor
towards the children's noise

her stomach rebels
      no lumpy porridge
could she swallow
dry toast her only repast

the sun casts pale shadows
on darkened windows
cars with headlights blazing
follow in procession

someone pulls her arm
propels her to the coffin
she touches the cold flesh
gags at her mother's painted face

Requiem - Jo Tregellis

how cold
the shoulder
you show me
the gaze
you bestow
the limp hand
you extend to me

how cold
your heart
to reject me

how cold
your grave will be
with no one
to tend it

Icy Voice – linda ruth brooks

November rain
soft and warm
unlike September's
cold stings

a hope
a flickering candle
slow careful words
precisely placed

a trap
a poisoned chalice

November rain
soft and warm
birdsong celebrates
Heaven's tears of joy

words of ash
I am no one you know

I Wonder - Rina Robinson

That day he said,
"I will get the car out.
I can go where I like.
I can do
what I like
with it then."

Is this
what he was thinking
when
he backed the car
out of the garage,
straight into me
a month ago.

A Child Remembers - Gail Hennessy

told on the bus home from school
'you don't belong'

nothing is as cold as charity
graven on the heart of the state ward.

holidays are especially stuffed when...
'How religion stuffs up holidays' - Jo Tregellis

HOLIDAYS & RELIGION

How Religion Stuffs up Holidays - Jo Tregellis

holidays were holy days
so it follows without religion
there would be no holidays

religions celebrate their origin
their god their rites their saints
followers are fanatics
drunk with the fervour
of their own righteousness
ever imbibing the teachings
ever obeying the rules of faith

holidays are especially stuffed
when christmas day and sunday
for example fall on different days
of the same week

plan your holiday
away from the holydays

Nothing But Crucifixions 'Til Tuesday - linda ruth brooks

Easter - three days or two?
they keep changing the dates
Coles and Woolworth's a zoo
tots clamouring for "choc'lates!"

my viewing pleasure
disappears in the fray
the telly has no treasure
just crucifixions 'til Tuesday

>	agony a religion?
>	a conundrum indeed
>	a sad substitution
>	for spiritual need
>
>	one day of sacrifice
>	one day of demise
>	one day should suffice
>	for humanity's prize
>
>	three plus years of humility
>	denouncing ignorance
>	pleasing religion a futility
>	Christ accused of 'tolerance'
>
>	agony fills coffers
>	puts bums on pews
>	that's what religiosity offers
>	paying altruism no dues

Easter is a Bunny
with a capital B
choccy treats from Nanny
two feet tall or three

resurrection day is 'other'
the neighbour kid's had a feed
then throws up on his mother
he's got a virus called Greed

Choices - Rina Robinson

An angel came to me one day, he said,
"You know why I am here,"
"Of course." I replied, "you've come for me
But I didn't know I was dead."

"You're not" he said, "I'm just a guide,
A forerunner to give you a choice.
Would you like to go fast or slow?"
I could hardly find my voice.

I never knew I would be asked to choose
The manner of my death
And so I gave no thought at all,
I merely held my breath.

Then I chose to go quite slowly,
The angel bowed his head,
"I'll see you later in years to come
When you are really dead."

So what did I do with those extra years
Did I make a few lives better?

I went back to my old way of life
Didn't even send Mum a letter.

Did I use my money for charitable works
Or for research into causes of pain?

Now my quality of life is all downhill
Would I make the same choice again.

I Remember - l.e. berry

i.
mum mum   when are we going

        god comes first,
        once we've been to church

do we have to
doesn't he say – ask and you shall receive
so I've asked can we go now

        it doesn't work that way
        effort first – then
        trust he'll look after you

mum, mum

        I hope you're packed
        so we can leave from the church

mum, mum
Sally's got my book
won't give it back

        don't forget god's watching
        you do want to have a great holiday
        remember to be nice to each other

but mum

        enough

ii.
        along the road ahead
        almost stationary cars
        create a lengthy ribbon

what's going on
why aren't we moving

        keep quiet
        be thankful I made you go to church
        or you might be the one
        under the load from the overturned truck

We too lend our tears
'While Broad Willows Weep' - linda ruth brooks

OBSERVE

While Broad Willows Weep – linda ruth brooks

The heart remembers what the mind forgets.
There is no sorrow deeper than the sorrow of unknowing
the sorrow of a truth denied.
While broad willows weep we too lend our tears
for those who travelled alone
their childhood innocence stolen
waiting for the heartache of generations
to be acknowledged   shared.
There are many to blame
systems, departments, churches
but ultimately people
their eyes closed   ears covered
to the voiceless
abandoned, abused and forgotten.
It could have been us
but it was you.
And it is you we will thank
survivors all
for finding courage
for bringing outrage.
For hanging on when the nation let go
for speaking when the world was silent.
We applaud you, celebrate and
remember you.

A Woman's Lot - l.e. berry
Influenced by 'Persuasion' - Jane Austen

Anne bowed to convention
Collective wisdom of ancestors
Decreed that age not youth
Arbiter of what love means

Under the shadow of mankind
She's cajoled how to think   to act   to behave
Unladylike emotions   suppressed
Boredom accepted as one's lot

Books   a genteel escape
Into a   foreign and exotic world
Unattainable for single females
Nearly thirty years of age

Anne learnt from heavy tomes
Women's views had an audience
From Biblical times to the present
Her sex once ruled society

But with no money
No wish to be an outcast
Her hands smoothed away wrinkles
Her nose twitched at beauty's smell

Her world held another challenge
For a heart stretched and bruised
Her lost love loved another
Bowed   she strove for acceptance

In a comedy of errors
Fate manipulated the actors
Threw them into the skies until
They land on their allotted square

The Space is Created - Jo Tregellis

a jangling saw
forces me to look.
the tree lopper
swings from umbilical ropes
safe-anchored and handcuffed
to the noise.

each severed branch
avoids the house,
a house built too close to the tree,
the tree that dares to drop leaves
on lawns and harbours birds
whose droppings whiten the path.

now the space is created.
no more shade
or blossom fall
winds must rustle and whoosh
in boughs farther on
birds must re-orient
their flight path
and must rebuild
in unfamiliar boughs.

I walk to the stump
no disease no termites
the proud scribbly gum
sawn into circles
its last eucalyptus scent
sharpening the evening air.

Blind Spot - Rina Robinson

Can't they see

Those nations that engage in wars
When all that is left is devastation and ruins
The people who triumph are the makers of weapons,
Nobody else wins
                                    Can't they see that?

Can't they see

The neighbours who bear a grudge
Have a constant foe when they could have a friend
Add to hostility and hate in the world
They simply lose in the end
                                    Can't they see that?

Can't they see

The persons assaulting their spouse
Who use conflict and injury to prove they are boss
Throw away the love that is everyone's right
It's always a constant loss
                                    Can't they see that?

Can't they see

Those people who abuse their child
Teach that violence is the way to live one's life
And that adults are cowards who think they are conquerors
It's never transient strife
                                    Can't they see that?

Chained – linda ruth brooks

short was his freedom
long was his chain
light at first
then heavy with strain

short his elation
long his despair
brief his enchantment
without a care

sweet the illusion
of leaving behind;
strong the delusion
peace his to find

sad the conclusion
to his swift farewell
leaving a master
with dread tales to tell

soft his return
harsh was the penalty
the chain confined him
ensuring captivity

bitter his repentance
silent his plea
slavery his lot
never to be free

haunting the music
lightly defined
           the organ grinder's monkey
           forever confined

strafed beneath a veil of unshed tears...
'What Comes from Above' – Gail Hennessy

VIEW

What Comes from Above - Gail Hennessy

It is mostly rain that falls from the skies
we know it for drops of water, ice cold
to the soft sibilance of snow.

It is manna from heaven
grain melded, our daily bread,
threshed from sun and soil.

These though are fashioned for destruction
Reaper and Predator, designed to home
in on the target, 'state of the art'

accuracy their benchmark of efficiency.

For those who operate
from the Nevada desert,
a new weapon of war homing in –

so much more effective
at preventing post traumatic
stress disorder - for the deliverer.

The enemy a blur on the screen
liquidated 'over there' not combat
hand to hand, but targeted killing.

To miss is failure,
success a bullseye precision.

Look to the heavens for this new gift
no cargo cult breaching the enemy walls
with strings of beads, a mirror for reflections.

Consider lives saved
when war can be waged
with victims in sight; out of mind

strafed beneath a veil of unshed tears...

Hidden Depths - l.e. berry

eyes downcast
she edges
along the footpath

onlookers wish she'd wash

she scans the street
hesitates   crosses the intersection
her footsteps quicken
as music blares from underground

as she peers inside
her shoulders slump
she resumes her search
for something lost

a man sidles up to her
hands open in supplication
she stops   reaches into her coat
turns out her pockets

empties nothing onto the ground

he slouches away
as another approaches
tries to remove warmth from
her thin shoulders

she pulls away   shrieks
it's all I've got between
me and the elements

you won't last the night
he sneers   *I want it*
she pulls the coat tighter
eyes flick around the street

with a turn of speed
that belies her appearance
she runs out of sight

He Thinks I Sleep – linda ruth brooks

He thinks I sleep through his morning ruminations
but I measure his every sound   my body straining
the muffled moan   the leaden footfall,
the long shower   mist escaping under the door
opening and closing of the fridge
the zipping of his school bag

he finds the note I wrote at 2 am
'have a good day, love Mum'
he shuffles past my door
I stay in my room
not cocooned in sleep
as he thinks

My muscles battle to relax
but I cannot rest   not yet
I do not go to him
If I do he will find it harder
to face the day
harder to leave

She is the mother, he thinks
I must tell her how hard all this is
'I don't want to go, don't make me go'
'Let me stay here with you'
'You don't know what it is like in that hell!'
'Now go, you will miss your bus'

He will engage me in a battle he must win
he must face the world without me
if I go to him I will hear of aches and fears
injuries and bullies, boredom and dread
and I will murmur about responsibility
of the future, of bravery and pride

And then he will sigh
'I do this for you, you know'
'Do it for you,' I will say
He will shrug into the day ahead
cutting the last thread
of connection and go

But if I stay in here warm in my bed
the sounds will be muffled
his courage easier to find
he will remember that he has to go
I hear the low slow burr of the sliding door open
and then close

I see him in my mind's eye
shoulders rounded
by the cares of his world
old black hat jammed
on his dark curly head
hair the image of mine at his age

I hear the swing of the gate
he is leaving to fight the dragons
in his kingdom once more
to school   to try again.
'I'm trying so hard Mum'
'I know'

He's gone now
my body slowly sighs
I sink deeply
into my marshmallow bed
I drift
sleep finds me

Blowin' in the Wind - Gail Hennessy

Dear Scarlett,

You were a bit of an inspiration
with your Southern Belle charm
the way you fought
like a vixen for "Tara"

the anti-heroine
such an antidote to
those Hollywood antiseptic stars.

But to be honest
it was the green dress
that won me
such 'make-do' pragmatism
a gown fit for a queen
fashioned from velveteen curtains
with yellow cord-pulls at the waist.

I was a bit disillusioned though
when I read on Google
of the labour intensity
200 hours of dressmaking skill
for the transformation

when I'd always assumed
it was a bit of stitch and tuck
so that Vivian Leigh could waltz
into Clark Gable's arms,
not a whole studio sweatshop
required behind the scenes

and I remember it scarlet
and now find it was green
because the director wanted
to match your eyes or tone
in with them at least.

But I did see that replica of "Tara"
in Charles Street, New Orleans
and I saw too the slave graves down South
with the wind blowing memory somewhere.

The Direction of Art - Rina Robinson

In the eye of the beholder
There is colour
There is line
Perhaps something more
To stir the imagination

In Modern Times
Paintings may take
The form of a Dream
Some may say
A Nightmare

But always
There is colour
There is line
And some imagination

It is impossible
To predict the future

One hopes
It is not
The Market
That forces
all Artists
To confirm
To Mediocrity

TANKA

Japanese in origin, a tanka is an unrhymed verse form of five lines originally containing five, seven, five, seven, and seven syllables respectively, but as Japanese syllables are different from English syllables, it has become acceptable to have a short line, a long line, a short line, and two long lines with about 32 syllables containing a subtle twist in its centre. The tanka takes us from delight to fulfilment, from insight to comprehension, and from the spontaneous to the measured. Traditionally tankas do not have titles.

Rina Robinson

a full busy day
many tasks before
the heat of summer
cool clean sheets on a soft bed
beckon tonight more than ever

morning message
sunlit crystals
glisten on spring grass
clearly nature surpasses
the magic of Merlin

Gail Hennessy

this doctor
young enough to be my grandson
what can he know
of the mysteries of healing-
of the heart's slow anguish

I glide
in my handsome wheelchair
a friend says
it's the colour of my first bike
more like a Harley really

l.e. berry

we inspect food
searching for a blemish
to reject it,
yet expect others
to overlook our failings

your eyes crinkle
at my approach ...
a memory that fades
as I tend your grave
on this windswept hill

Jo Tregellis

as kids we hop scotched
jumped the dizzy numbers
on the footpath
my shiny taw
kept under my pillow

reality
exists outside his mind -
a boy
at the baker's window
fumbles in empty pockets

linda ruth brooks

breath of eve'ning
touches my secret heart
to its depths
it's your birthday
do you remember me

how long will you stay
all I have to offer you
is constant love
what reason will keep you near
you're already gone

ANSWERS TO RIDDLE POEMS
on pages 37-39

The Flu	linda ruth brooks
Lily of the Valley	Jo Tregellis
Snow	Gail Hennessy
Breath	l.e. berry
Bicycle Helmet	Rina Robinson

CENTO SOURCES FOR POEMS

Loss – Rina Robinson

1 Hardy, *At Castle Boterel*
2 Browning, *Epilogue to Aselando*
3 Cotton, *Laura sleeping*
4 Byron, *She walks in Beauty*
5 Yeats, *Byzantium*
6 Yeats, *Long legged Fly*
7 Hardy, *After the Visit*
8 Marlow, *The Passionate Shepherd*
9 Ralegh, *To Scinthia*
10 Shakespeare, *Lament Cymbeline*
11 Hardy, *The Voice*
12 Rochester, *A Song*
13 Patmore, *A Farewell*
14 Hopkins, *Heaven Haven*
15 Campion, *Third Book of Airs*
16 Graves, *Full Moon*
17 Landor, *Ianthe*
18 Lovelace, *To Anthea from Prison*
19 Shelley, *A Song*
20 Christina Rossetti, *A Pause for Thought*
21 Browning, *Two in the Campagna*
22 Masefield, *The Gift Outright*
23 Rochester, *A Song*
24 Emerson, *Hymn*
25 Patmore, *A Farewell*
26 Wyatt, *A Renouncing of Love*

Written on the Sky - Gail Hennessy

1-2 Jack Gilbert, *Tear It Down*
3-4 Charles Wright, *Body and Soul II*
5 Judith Wright, *Remittance Man*
6 Eavan Boland, *The Pomegranate*
7-8 Rachel Eliza Griffiths *28*
9 Dylan Thomas, *In My Craft or Sullen Art*
10-11 Linda Gregg, *We Manage Most When We Manage Small*
12 Mark Tredinnick, *The Margaret River Sestets*
13 Jack Gilbert, *Tear It Down*
14 Judith Beveridge, *Bahadour*

No Retreat - l.e. berry

1. Bruce Penn, *The Voice*
2. Bruce Penn, *Reflection*
3. Norma Knight, *Balancing*
4. Louise Oxley, *Glove*
5. Andrew Sant, *Lineage*
6. Peter Hay, *Caucasian Haiku*
7. Chloe Munro, *Draw a Frame around It*
8. David Kirkby, *Weston*
9. Anne Kellas, *Following Iacris*
10. Sue Moss, *Homage to Betty Canter*
11. Adrienne Eberhard, Absence
12. Karen Knight, *Like Most Sunday*
13. Liz Winfield, *Bicarbonate Soda Water*
14. Liz Winfield, *Dear Eric*
15. Robyn Mathison, *Sunday Solstice*

A Warm Wind - Jo Tregellis

1 Walter De La Mare, *Song of the Mad Prince*
2 Rupert Brooke, *The Hill*
3 William Blake, *And Did Those Feet in Ancient Time*
4 George Gordon, Lord Byron, *There is a Pleasure in the Pathless Woods*
5 T S Eliot, *East Coker*
6 T S Eliot, *East Coker*
7 Thomas Hardy, *Weather*
8 Thomas Hardy, *Weather*
9 Gerard Manley Hopkins, *As Kingfishers Catch Fire, Dragonflies Draw Flame*
10 John Masefield, *The West Wind*
11 John Masefield, *The West Wind*
12 Rudyard Kipling, *The Betrothed*
13 Rudyard Kipling, *The Betrothed*
14 William Shakespeare, *A Midsummer Night's Dream*
15 William Shakespeare, *A Midsummer Night's Dream*
16 Dorothy Parker, *Not So Deep as a Well*
17 Dorothy Parker *Not So Deep as a Well*
18 Cornelius Whur *The Female Friend*
19 Cornelius Whur *The Female Friend*

False Love – linda ruth brooks

1,2 Alexander Pope *Epistle to a Young Lady...*
3   Lord Tennyson *The Lotus-Eaters*
4   Robert Frost *The Death of the Hired Man*
5   Lord Tennyson *Morte d'Arthur*
6   Robert Frost *Birches*
7   Samuel Taylor Coleridge *The Rime of the Ancient Mariner*
8   William Blake *Broken Love*
9   Ella Wheeler Cox *Love's coming*
10,11 Oscar Wilde *Roses and Rue*
12,13 William Butler Yeats *Never Give all the Heart*
14,15 William Shakespeare *A Lover's Complaint*
16,17 Emily Dickenson *Love's Stricken 'why'*
18,19 John Keats *Ode to a Nightingale*
20   Kenneth Slessor *Five Bells*
21   W. H. Auden *Lullaby*
22   Elizabeth Browning *A woman's shortcomings*

POETS

l. e. berry

l.e. berry (Louise Berry) has had poems published in various anthologies including *Central Coast Poets, People of the Valley* and *Wood Brick and Stone* (commended), *Eucalypt, Poetry at the Pub* anthologies, *Women's Work, Food for Thought, Grevillea & Wonga Vine,* and *We are Australians*. She is past President of Central Coast Poets, a member of Hunter Writers' Centre poetry group, a member of Hunter FAW, and co-ordinates Third Wednesday Poets, and Fourth Tuesday Poets.

Always Sceptical	3
A Different Hue	8
The End is Nigh	18
Last Solstice?	20
No Retreat	26
Lady in the Garden	30
Unbroken Bond	32
Riddle poem	38
So Sorry	53
Water's Memory	59
Us or Them	69
So Cold	72
I Remember	83
A Woman's Lot	87
Hidden Depths	93
Tanka	102

o   Tanka; *Food for Thought* - Ginninderra Press
o   Tanka; *Eucalypt* - Issue 8, 2010

linda ruth brooks

linda ruth brooks: writer, artist and former registered nurse is best known for her childhood memoir *A Curious & Inelegant Childhood*. She has also published fiction novels and written and illustrated children's books and writes regularly for the local Gazette. Her poetry has been published in *We are Australian, Seeking the Sun* and various newspapers. She has been a member of Third Wednesday Poets since 2011. www.lindaruthbrooks.com

Election	5
Leaves	12
Finis	16
False Love	28
Light	33
Riddle Poem	39
Chasm	45
Tsunami	54
They Were...	63
Dream Holiday	66
Icy Voice	75
Nothing But Crucifixions Til Tuesday	81
While Broad Willows Weep	86
Chained	90
He Thinks I Sleep	94
Tanka	104

- *Leaves* – 'Seeking the Sun' (Central Coast Poets Inc.)
- *While broad willows weep* 'We are Australian'
- *He thinks I sleep* 'I'm not broken, I'm just different' (nonfiction book on Asperger's Syndrome)

Gail Hennessy

Gail Hennessy's poetry has been widely published in literary journals, national and regional newspapers and anthologies since the 1970s. She was an active member and prize winner in the Society of Women Writers in Canberra in the 1980s. After an extended period of academic study, which resulted in a doctorate in Australian studies, she has returned to writing poetry in Newcastle, participating in branches of the FAW and as a member of the Hunter Writers Centre. In 2009 she published a collection of published and new poems, 'Witnessing', many drawing on her thesis. In her own words 'as a member of the third Wednesday poets I enjoy sharing a mutual love for writing poetry in all its forms'.

9/11	4
Found	10
The Mayan Prophecy	22
Written on the Sky	25
Gauguin's Visit	34
Riddle poem	38
Korowa - Celebration Trees at the Ocean Baths	42
Poppies	52
Home	56
Change of Season	60
The Gang	67
A Child Remembers	77
What Comes from Above	92
Blowin' in the Wind	96
Tanka	101

- *Change of Season* honourable mention in Kathryn Purnell competition, Society of Women Writers, 2012 .
- *Gauguin's Visit* winning poem FAW Eastwood-Hills Free Verse competition, 2012.
- *Home* 'Witnessing' 2009 and in Sydney University Alumni Magazine, 2011.
- *Korowa - Trees at the Ocean Baths*, winning poem 'Wood, Brick and Stone', Catchfire Press, 2011.
- *Poppies* winning poem 'People of the Valley', Catchfire Press 2009, and in 'Witnessing' 2009.

Rina Robinson

Rina Robinson has published fantasy novels, fiction, short stories; and written and illustrated children's poetry books. Rina's poetry has been published in 'We are Australian', 'Yellow Moon', anthologies by 'Catchfire Press' and various magazines.

Just for the Moment	6
Red and Gold	9
Echoes	13
Life is Chaos, Chaos is Life	19
Loss	24
Picasso	36
Riddle Poem	38
Nature's Gift	47
Sad Yesterdays	58
Dawn's Glory	62
I Wonder	76
Choices	82
Blind Spot	89
A Direction of Art	97
Tanka	100

- *Sad Yesterdays* 'Views & Visions'
- *Blind spot* 'Views & Visions'

Jo Tregellis

Jo (Josephine) Tregellis is a writer of free verse, traditional verse, tanka, haiku, short stories and the occasional article. Her work is published in journals and anthologies including *Yellow Moon, Eucalypt- a tanka journal,* six Catchfire Press anthologies (co-editor of three), *Third Australian Haiku Anthology, We are Australian, Food for Thought, The Melody lingers On, Wind Over Water,* and others. Some poems have been published in the United States and Japan. Born and educated in Newcastle, Jo is now a resident of Lake Macquarie. She is a member of Hunter Fellowship of Australian Writers, Catchfire press committee, Bowerbird Tanka Group and Third Wednesday Poets. Her main interests are everything Australian and listening to classical piano music.

Waiting for Wednesday Poets	2
Seasons of the Trees	11
World's End	17
A Warm Wind	27
Sunday Girls	31
New York Movie	35
Riddle Poem	39
In the High Country	44
Scarlet	46
Pulbah Speaks	50
Sonnet on Death	61
One View of Australia	68
Requiem	74
How Religion Stuffs up Holidays	80
The Space is Created	88
Tanka	103

- *Seasons of the trees*; 'We are Australian' 2010
- *The space is created*; Awarded first place in Macarthur FAW's 2007 free verse competition.
- *Pulbah Speaks*; Through the Valley, 2007
- Tanka - *as kids*; Eucalypt issue7, 2009
- *Reality;* Wind Over Water, 2009

www.ingramcontent.com/pod-product-compliance
Lightning Source LLC
Chambersburg PA
CBHW031424290426
44110CB00011B/510